The Power
to Navigate Your Destiny

The Five Essential Principles You Need
to Access the Power Within

DR. THERESA POUSSAINT

ARCHWAY
PUBLISHING

Archway Publishing books may be ordered through booksellers or by contacting:

Archway Publishing
1663 Liberty Drive
Bloomington, IN 47403
www.archwaypublishing.com
844-669-3957

Because of the dynamic nature of the Internet, any web addresses or
links contained in this book may have changed since publication and
may no longer be valid. The views expressed in this work are solely those
of the author and do not necessarily reflect the views of the publisher,
and the publisher hereby disclaims any responsibility for them.

Any people depicted in stock imagery provided by Getty Images are
models, and such images are being used for illustrative purposes only.
Certain stock imagery © Getty Images.

Scripture taken from the King James Version of the Bible.

ISBN: 978-1-4808-9793-9 (sc)
ISBN: 978-1-4808-9794-6 (e)

Library of Congress Control Number: 2020920471

Print information available on the last page.

Archway Publishing rev. date: 01/04/2021

To all women, especially my daughters, Cordelia and Felicity, who are my inspiration. My hope is to empower you and give you the tools you need to embrace your lives and circumstances and take control of your destinies.

Control your own destiny or someone else will.

Anonymous

Contents

Principle Five - Persevere: *DON'T* Give Up

The race is not given to the swift nor
the strong, but to he who endures until the end.

Acknowledgements

I want to dedicate this book to those who have gone on before me:

My ex-husband, Andre' Maximillian Poussaint

My parents, Bishop Ellihue and Mother Janie Cartledge

My brothers, Howard and Willie Cartledge

My sisters, Rose Parker and Laura Holman

My mentor, Roy Seavy Campbell

Additional mentors:

> Susan Aldridge, PhD
>
> Michael Frank, PhD
>
> Leslie Dinauer, PhD
>
> Richard Granat, Esq.
>
> Lucille McCorkle

Introduction

I am not famous. I am not rich. I don't have the resources celebrities have in order to propel their books to the *New York Times* best sellers list. I am an unknown, average, divorced mother of two. I have had my fair share of being knocked down in life, and I have sometimes struggled to get back up. I wrote this book to offer five proven principles that helped me to overcome obstacles during my marriage, separation, and ultimate divorce. The obstacles included depression, loneliness, mental fatigue, and the economic challenges of being the head of a household when it was just me and my two daughters. These principles enabled me to flourish and reach my personal and professional goals.

I hope that, by sharing my story, I will empower women who feel that they have no control over their lives—women who wonder every day how they will get through the next; who feel as if life has not dealt them a fair hand; or who have questioned themselves and, at times, God. This book is for you. I want to help you realize that you can take control of your life, develop and execute a plan, finish what you started, and reap the rewards of all of your hard work. I wrote this book because I believe that, if you look deep within, you will see that you are strong, you are brave, you can accomplish anything, and most of all, you have *The Power to Navigate Your Destiny*.

Planted

For as long as I can remember, I've wanted nothing more than to teach. On my first day of kindergarten, I walked into Mrs. Wilkerson's classroom. When I saw the bright primary colors of the ABC posters lining the walls, and her comforting smile welcoming me, I felt safe; that is, until I realized my mother wouldn't be staying with me. I cried. I cried and begged her to stay until Mrs. Wilkerson said, "She will be back later to pick you up, but until then we have some learning to do."

Learning always excited me. I read constantly as a child. Picture books, chapter books, the Bible—any book that was put in front of me I devoured. When I was ten, my dad, who was a minister, made me the Sunday school teacher for the little children at our church. I showed up on my first Sunday with index cards filled with biblical stories such as Noah's Ark and Adam and Eve. I used these cards as I coached the children to present the story at the end of Sunday school to the congregation.

When I was fifteen, my dad allowed me to begin teaching the adults. I developed activities and exercises in order to make learning fun for them. I was excited to be able to have deeper conversations about the Bible and expand on what I had done with the children. During one Sunday school class, I gave a quiz to test the adults on scriptures—the Old Testament as well as the New Testament. Once

I collected the quizzes, I saw that well over half of them were blank. Afterwards, I asked one of the congregates, Gertrude, why she hadn't finished the quiz. She looked at me, sadness filling her eyes, and said "Sister, I can't read. I only know a few words." That night, remembering that look in her eyes, I knew what God had put me on this earth to do. God put me here to teach. I had found my purpose.

I loved school and was regularly one of the top students in my class. I always held teachers in high regard and believed they positively impacted my desire to also teach.

When I was in high school, I found it difficult to fit in. I was not popular, and I did not have the same friends I had at my elementary and middle schools. Feeling out of place, I decided to focus on my academics, since that was the part of school, I was better at anyway. I also joined the high school band as a majorette. Being a majorette was amazing. Suddenly I fit in with ease, and I had friends who were popular.

During my senior year, my chemistry teacher, Mrs. McCorkle whom I loved, began encouraging me to apply to colleges. I was surprised at the suggestion, since our guidance counselor tried to discourage me from going to college at all. Even though I was an honor student, no one ever encouraged me to go to college until Mrs. McCorkle advised me.

No one in my family had gone to college; for me it wasn't even thought of as a feasible path. The fact that I was about to finish high school was an accomplishment and something to be proud of. My parents had nine children, and I was the youngest. While there was always enough to go around, there wasn't much extra. I was expected to graduate and get a job, but instead I took Mrs. McCorkle's advice.

I was accepted into College of Wooster in Ohio with a partial scholarship. Since the scholarship was only partial, I told my parents they were responsible for the rest of the tuition, and though it would be tough, they agreed to make it work.

When I arrived on campus, I was stunned – culture shocked. I had spent my childhood in Washington DC, back then affectionately named "Chocolate City." For my entire life, I had gone to schools in which the majority of kids were black; here I was one in a handful out of thousands.

After a few classes, I quickly realized that my public education could not be compared to the preparatory schools that most of my classmates had come from. I was intimidated and had to get used to working much harder than I did in high school. At the end of my first semester, I did well even though I did not achieve the straight A's I was accustomed to. I went home for winter break excited and proud to share with my parents all I had learned.

During the final week of winter break, I got a phone call from the college. I was told that my tuition hadn't been paid, and I would not be allowed to attend classes starting the following week. I was heartbroken. My parents simply didn't have the money to pay the remainder of the tuition. I was angry at them and extremely sad. My achievements were something I was incredibly proud of, and to have that educational opportunity snatched away hurt beyond belief.

Though I was upset, I understood my parent's finances and how they had sacrificed to send me to school for the first semester. So instead of driving back to school and starting classes, I got a job.

Growing

I was working for a law school for a couple of years and was promoted to the position of registrar. Shortly thereafter the school was going through some financial difficulties and sought to be acquired. The staff was told to prepare for a visit from an investor. One day a man approached me. "What's your name?" he asked.

"Hi, I'm Theresa, but everyone calls me Tee."

"Hello, my name is Richard, but don't call me Dick," he said with a smile.

Richard was an attorney businessman who was appointed overseer of an unaccredited law school in the city. The law school was ordered to phase out the currently enrolled students by helping them to finish up there or get into other law schools that were accredited. After I explained to Richard and one of his human resource people what I did as the registrar for the law school, he was impressed and looked at me and said, "You come with me."

I was young, in my early twenties, and eager to learn. Richard taught me so much about the administrative side of running a school. He encouraged me to go back to college and offered to pay my tuition. This was indeed a blessing because the only reason I was not in college was that I did not have the financial means to pay for it. So, without hesitation, I enrolled and began taking courses during the evening toward a college degree.

The phase-out of the law school was a success. Soon after its completion, Richard acquired a paralegal school in Philadelphia and asked me if I would relocate to help him run the school. He needed me to help him apply for financial aid administration through the Department of Education for his newly acquired school.

Shortly after I moved to the new big city, I met Max on the trolley I rode every day to and from work. One evening, after saying good-bye to the trolley driver, I got off at my stop. As I was walking toward my apartment, a man walked up next to me and introduced himself. "Hi, I'm Andre' Maximillian Poussaint. How are you?"

"Hi. Just fine. How are you?"

"I'm great now that I have met you. What is your name?"

"My name is Theresa."

"Where are you from?" he asked.

"I'm from DC."

"Yes, I knew you weren't from here."

"How did you know I was not from here?"

"Well, I figured you were from out of town because most women from around here know about the reputation of these trolley drivers, and since you were so friendly with the guy, I assumed you just didn't know."

As we walked toward my apartment, we talked about our respective lines of work and discovered we lived in the same apartment complex. When we arrived at my building, he asked me for my phone number, and I obliged. He called me later that evening, and we talked on the phone for hours.

Max was a gentleman. He took me out on dates, including fine dining at a fancy French restaurant and showed me the finer things in life. He was different. He was classy and elegant. He was a musician with a classically trained baritone voice. He introduced me to classical music, and because he enjoyed it so much, I acquired a liking for it too. He taught me there is more than just hearing instruments—pipe organ, violin, cello, brass and percussions. He taught me the interpretation of the music of his favorite composer, Johann Sebastian Bach. He loved Baroque music. For example, we didn't enjoy Handel's Messiah just during the Christmas holiday season; we enjoyed it all year round.

It was a whirlwind courtship; things moved very fast. A few months before our wedding, we decided to get a penthouse apartment together. It was like Noah's Ark. We had two of everything— two ironing boards, two irons, two microwaves. One evening, I was working on a project and had to work late. When I finally arrived home, Max told me that the dinner he had prepared for me was in the microwave. I went to the microwave to see what he had prepared for dinner and, to my surprise, when I opened the microwave, I found a small box. I opened the box and found a one-and-a-half-carat marquis-cut diamond ring. As I stood there totally surprised with my mouth hanging open, he came up to me and asked me if I would marry him. I replied, "Yes!" We planned for an April wedding.

Just a few weeks before the wedding, we had a terrible argument over financing the wedding. My parents were unable to assist me in any way financially, so all of the financial burden rested on us. One evening, Max was driving my car, and he picked me up from work. On the way home, we started arguing about the cost of the wedding. The conversation got very heated. I don't even remember what I said, but whatever it was led to a behavior I never had witnessed from him before. He slapped me across my mouth! Blood gushed all over my white blouse. We were approaching a stop light, and as I was in shock from the hit, I immediately reached for the door handle and tried to get out of the car. He pulled me back in. I know people were looking, but because I was in shock, all I could think of was getting away from him.

When we pulled into the garage of our new penthouse apartment, he apologized profusely, but I was not paying him any attention. He tried to cover up my bloody blouse with his jacket before we got on the elevator because he did not want the doorman or concierge to see it. When we got upstairs to our apartment, I immediately retreated to the bedroom to think about what I was going to do. He kept apologizing and was remorseful, saying that he was sorry and it would never happen again. I was contemplating calling off the wedding, but I realized that all of the money we had put into the planning would be lost, and we had both just signed a two-year lease on the apartment. So, I felt stuck. I decided to accept his apology and not tell anyone about the incident—even my eldest brother, whom I knew would probably kill him, and I didn't want that to happen. My oldest brother would have defended his baby sister. So, I didn't tell anyone. I know that, if I had told anyone, he or she would probably have told me not to marry him. What did I learn from this? Women, don't be fooled! Without professional intervention or help, the abuse will happen again. And it did. More on that later.

The year was 1986 when I married the man of my dreams. He was tall, dark, and handsome—six foot four and 210 pounds. He was intelligent and cultured. Like most brides, I thought I would always be married to my husband and that we would grow old together. After all, my parents had been married for sixty years, so there was no doubt in my mind that I would do the same. I was committed and took my vows very seriously.

Although I was twenty-six years old when I got married, I was naïve. I did not fully understand that Max's behavior was just a symptom of something deeper. In hindsight, it was relative to his unhealthy relationship with his mother and his time serving in the military during wartime. When Max introduced me to his mother and other family members, on the surface, everyone appeared to get along. However, over time, I learned that his parents divorced when he was young—around six years old.

His father remarried and practically disowned him and his brother. He recalled that, at his father's funeral, he and his brother were not even recognized as his father's children. More attention was focused on his current wife and children. Max's mother remarried also, but according to Max she married a boxer who used him as a punching bag. When Max was a teenager, he excelled academically and was a gifted musician. He was not the typical boy involved in sports activities. His step-father resented that and gave Max a difficult time. Max ended up resenting his mother because she did not intervene. At the age of sixteen, Max decided to move out. He got a job at a restaurant and rented a room. Shortly thereafter, he enlisted in the US Navy.

I do remember that, when Max took me to his mother's house for dinner to introduce me to his family, I met his mother, his mother's boyfriend, and his sister and brother—the children of his step-father. They all seemed normal. Max made sure that the visit did not last too long. I don't think that had to do with me, but rather with his tolerance level of being around his family.

On April 26, 1986, Max and I were married in a beautiful church wedding. My family and closest friends came from out of town. It was a joyous occasion, and at the end of the day, we were so exhausted we did not make love on our wedding night. We did not go on a honeymoon because we had spent all of our money on the wedding. Since we had just moved into the penthouse apartment, it was new enough that it served as a great getaway. We simply enjoyed being together in our new home. I describe my fifteen-year marriage (living together as husband and wife) as 75 percent successful and sum it up like this—year one was the year of transitioning and adjusting, year seven was the seven-year itch, and years thirteen, fourteen, and fifteen were like pure hell. During years sixteen, seventeen, and eighteen we were separated and finally divorced.

Changing

Year One—The Adjustment Year

One of the things I liked so much about Max was his strength as a man. Every woman wants a strong man—not a weak man. However, a man must learn how to balance his strength when he is dealing with a woman. He needs to make sure that he is not overpowering and downright controlling the woman. That is what the issue was in the first year.

Instead of getting to know me as a woman, and understanding my ways and thought process, Max tried to control my ways, thoughts, views, and opinions. He would ask, "Why do you do that?" or "Why did you say that?"

"Ahh, because." Would be my response. "What do you mean why? Why do I have to explain why? It is simply because it's me. Don't try to change me. Let me be me. Let my thoughts be my thoughts. I do not want to be like you. I want to be me." Because of this conflict, we had many arguments, and I often wondered if I had made the right choice to marry him. I often reflected on the slapping incident that happened before the wedding. Too late. It had been my decision to marry him. As my mother would say, "You made the bed, now you have to lie in it."

Written by Dr. Theresa Poussaint

One argument turned violent when he shoved me onto the bed when I was pregnant. Another turned violent when I was holding our infant daughter. I don't understand why a man his size would hit or shove a woman. Every time he physically abused me, I would privately wish that another man would kick his ass so that he could feel what I felt. I think that men who abuse women are cowards and need someone to kick their asses so that they can think twice before assaulting a woman again.

Again, I purposefully did not tell my family, especially my oldest brother because he would have traveled to Philadelphia, killed Max, and asked questions later. He was indeed a hothead, so instead of seeing my brother spend the rest of his life in prison, I just didn't say anything. I figured it was my marriage, and I had to deal with it the best way I could.

The following years were better. We shared some great times and great moments. We had our first daughter, Cordelia, on December 31, New Year's Eve. She brought so much joy into our lives. Perhaps we just fell into the routine of getting along. I learned to pick my battles. I supported his many business ventures, and we attended his Episcopalian church as a family. I have a solid foundation of Christianity learned from being a Pentecostal preacher's kid (PK) and was open to learn about other religions.

My father often said from the pulpit that he could send his baby girl to any church and she would come back the same. She is not wavered by other philosophies and beliefs; she clearly understands her religious roots. He often recalls when I attended the late Daddy Grace and Daddy McCullough's church for a gospel concert. During the service, the congregation was singing "Daddy's on the Main Line." Well, in my church we say, "Jesus is on the Main Line." I realized they were acknowledging that "Daddy McCullough" was their Jesus. Daddy McCullough was very light skinned—almost white. When he entered, we all stood, and everyone began to bow and cheer. As he strolled to the pulpit, two little black girls came to his side with hand fans and began to fan him. He did not say a word and only made gestures. He slightly elevated his hand to indicate that the master of ceremony could continue. It was as if he was a god of some sort. I was amazed and flabbergasted because I had never seen a man treated as a deity—like God on earth, like the pope. The Bible tells us that God is a spirit and those who worship him must worship him in spirit and in truth, so I knew that Daddy McCullough was no God, just like I know the pope is no God. They are human men. But it appeared as though I may have been the only person in this church who felt this way. It was an eye-opening experience. I remember coming home and telling my father about this experience and that was when he said that he could send me anywhere and I would not come back changed or confused.

So, attending an Episcopalian church was new to me, but I was not afraid to experience something different. The church was much different than mine. It was more pompous and ceremonial with incense, candles, and chants. The priest was more of a speaker than a preacher. However, as long as I was in the house of the Lord, I was good.

Year Seven—The Seven-Year Itch

There were still times when things would get out of hand and we would argue. I was resolved to have my own identity, and I refused to let someone dictate to me how I should feel or what I should say. Again, just let me be me. I decided to go back to school and get the college degree I longed for. I called my best friend, Patricia, the maid of honor at my wedding, and asked her to loan me money to buy books to start school. I told her I would repay her once my financial aid went through. She wired the money to me, and I was able to start classes at the local community college. I had planned out the next two years of classes to earn an associate's degree. I figured I would take it one step at a time—one semester at a time.

In the meantime, another argument turned violent. One day Max came home from work and I was cooking dinner. He was in a bad mood and began to argue with me. Again, I do not remember what the argument was about, but I did speak up and began arguing back at him. I was in the kitchen and he was in the bedroom. I was bending over getting something out of the refrigerator when all of a sudden, his hands were around my neck. He choked me and I saw complete blackness for a second or two. He let go and I was coughing and in shock. I realized how close I was to death. He almost killed me. Again, I told no one about the incident. There are so many women just like me who have been and who are abused in silence. I was lucky that he did not hold on any longer than he did. God was truly covering me and watching over my life.

Max had graduated from college, so I assumed he was an advocate of higher education. I assumed wrong. He believed in higher education, but just did not want me to get a degree. He told me that I was his wife and needed to be home taking care of his child. Getting my degree was a personal mission for me, and I did not feel I needed his approval. One day he came home from work and saw my books on the table. "What is this?" he asked. I told him I was enrolled in school. He was not happy and said, "All I know is, my dinner had better be on the table when I get home from work." I told him that I would make sure that it would be and that I would also make sure that I did well in school. I have always had a thirst for knowledge and loved to learn. So, I knew that I would thrive in a learning environment. Education is empowering, and a liberal arts education offers the breadth and depth of knowledge anyone needs. I had so many "aha" moments in my psychology and sociology classes that I began to understand human behavior on an intellectual level.

About half way through the academic year, I went to my sociology class, and as usual, I sat on the front row. My professor immediately noticed a change in my attitude and inquired why I was looking upset. I told him that I was a bit upset because I had just learned that I was pregnant. And that this meant that the pursuit of my degree would again be taking a detour. I had tried several times before to earn my degree, but life had got in the way. There may have been arguments along the way, but there was also making up along the way, and my second child was a surprise.

I attended school for as long as I could and then I had to stop to have the baby. I instantly bonded with our second daughter, Felicity, nursing her for twenty-three months. I believe I bonded with her so deeply because, as time went on, Max and I grew apart, and I needed someone to be close to.

Years Thirteen, Fourteen, and Fifteen—Like Pure Hell

I describe years thirteen, fourteen, and fifteen as pure hell because they were the most difficult years of my marriage. My husband told me that he hated me and that I was a no-good wife and mother. He knew just what buttons to push to take me to a low place. I may not have been the wife he wanted me to be, but I take the role of motherhood very seriously. He then told me that he would never touch me again. I know that these are mean things to say to a person, but he meant it, and he showed it in his actions and behavior towards me.

I worked during the day, and he worked the graveyard shift. We barely communicated, but I continued with my studies working toward completing my bachelor's degree. I took any negative thoughts and energy and turned them into positive thoughts and energy toward my education and my daughters. It was extremely difficult, but I prayed constantly for strength to get through it all. I would come home from work, prepare dinner, help the girls with their homework, do my schoolwork, and fall asleep on the sofa until he left for work at around eleven o'clock. I would then go to the bedroom to sleep and start the process all over again the next day.

He had built up so much hate for me, and it showed up one evening when we got into an argument. I can't even remember what the argument was about, but he raised his hands to hit me. I told him that, if he hit me, I was going to call the police, and he was going to go to jail. That scared him enough to pull back and rethink his attack. I had taken enough physical and mental abuse over the years. I was done with the situation and would not tolerate another episode. That event was the impetus he needed to want a divorce.

The Divorce

After fifteen years of marriage my husband called me at work and told me that he was leaving me. He had started the conversation by asking me questions about the balance on all of our accounts.

I had told him the balance on the mortgage and credit cards. He said he was asking me these questions because he was planning to leave me. I responded that he must be talking about leaving me physically because he had left spiritually and emotionally several years ago. Of course, I had been distraught but yet not surprised that my marriage was ending. I had just never thought I would be divorced.

Like most people who get married, my plan was to be married until death. I wanted to grow old with him. My parents served as role models to me in their marriage because they stood the test of time through good and bad, and ups and downs until my mother's death. But the handwriting was on the wall for me and my husband. We were like two ships passing in the night, working different schedules, so we barely communicated. I felt his disdain for me every day. I prayed and prayed that things would get better, but they never did. I never understood why he hated me so.

As a PK, I was raised with strong morals and values. I purposefully treat people the way I want to be treated. I was deeply in love with my husband and accepted that, if he became incapacitated due to his illness, I would have no problem taking care of him. But I realized that he would not do the same for me. I recommended counseling, but unfortunately, marriage counseling was not an option. Like many African American men in my culture, my husband did not take well to the concept of marriage counseling and having people involved in our marriage. He was an intelligent man, so perhaps he knew that it would put him in a vulnerable position, and he would have to confront the demons in his life, primarily his unhealthy relationship with his mother. Also, I think this fear originated from knowing the history of how black men were treated during times of slavery. Black men were bought and sold like pieces of meat. They were told what to do, when to do it, and how to do it. Today, many of them simply refuse to allow anyone (especially white men) to tell them how to live their lives. Call it fear or disdain, but it takes two people to mess up a marriage; thus, it will take two people to fix a marriage. One person cannot do it alone, so if marriage counseling is out of the question, then it is inevitable that the marriage will end.

When I got home one evening from work, we sat down and discussed how we were going to handle breaking the bad news to our two daughters, ages fourteen and six. Ironically, Max was just six years old when his parents divorced. We decided we would sell the house, split everything fifty-fifty, and go our separate ways. However, the one thing I made clear immediately was that the girls would come with me. I didn't care about furniture or other possessions; I could always replace them. But my strong maternal instinct took over to ensure the well-being of my daughters. We told the girls that we were separating, and although they were crying and upset about us splitting up, they were not surprised. It is amazing how kids already know that things are not good. They just didn't know how to comprehend it or how it would impact their lives, especially our six-year-old.

I know that there are many single and divorced moms who do a brave and heroic job on behalf of their kids. Still, children living with single mothers are five times more likely to be poor than children in two-parent households. Children in single-parent homes are also more likely to drop out of school and become teen parents, even when financial hardship is not an obstacle. Evidence suggests that, on average, children who live with both their biological mother and father have more stability in their lives than those who live in stepfamilies or with cohabitating partners. Knowing this, I was determined to beat the odds of these statistics. My two daughters became my focus and primary motivation.

Fortunately, I was only a few months from completing my bachelor's degree and would have greater potential to take care of my girls and myself. I knew that I had to complete my degree so that I could compete in the job market and move up at my place of work. About six months after we separated, Max told me that he wanted to reconcile and that my earning my degree was actually a threat to him. He thought I had been positioning myself to leave him. I guess after fifteen years of marriage Max didn't know me as well as I thought he should have. I was not positioning myself to leave him. I was positioning myself to become the primary breadwinner in the family due to his declining health issues associated with diabetes. Max had been diagnosed as a diabetic just three short months after we were married. Even though he has a medical background—he served as a corpsman in the US Navy during the Vietnam War (which I found out after his death that he was exposed to agent orange) and worked as a hospital administrator— he literally thought it was a death sentence. I comforted him and reassured him that it was not. At that time, my mother had been living with diabetes for over twenty years. It was important for him to take care of himself—to exercise, watch what he ate, and not smoke or drink alcohol.

I graduated from college, earning my bachelor's degree in communications studies. It was a joyous occasion that I was able to share with my parents and family. After so many years of starts and stops, it finally happened. I was the first family member to earn a college degree and wanted to be a role model not only to my daughters, but to my nineteen nieces and nephews. Consequently, our family now has four generations of college graduates.

As Max and I began to divide up our worldly possessions, we also decided to put the house up for sale and split our debts down the middle. He would take everything he brought into the marriage—he had some pretty nice furniture—and I would take most of the items we purchased together during the marriage. My primary concern were my daughters. I called my parents to ask them if the girls and I could come home and live with them until I was able to regroup and find a place for us. Of course, they said yes.

Ironically, as Max was preparing to move out, he needed me to be a cosigner on his apartment lease because he was not earning enough money to get into the apartment complex he desired. I agreed to cosign. I know you ask why would I do that? This man had just told me he was leaving me. Why would I do that for him? Perhaps because I am not a mean-spirited person. What woman cosigns on a lease for the husband who is leaving her? Seems crazy, but that is what I did. I am not a bitter person. I do not hold grudges. I do not hate people, even those who may hate me. It was also a way for me to ensure my daughters could be in a good and safe environment with their dad when they visited him. It would somehow later prove to be a wise choice.

My father later told me that it was the missionary in me and the biblical teachings, morals, and values that were a part of me that caused me to react the way I did in that situation. When I was young, I attended church all the time, sometimes seven days a week if we were having a revival. As a teenager, I did not like being in church all the time, but as an adult, I realized it was the best place for me. My church experience has grounded me, and my parents' teachings laid the foundation of my moral values and are the fabric of the woman I am today.

My husband made it very clear that he was not leaving our two daughters but that he was leaving *me*. I did not want to get a divorce. I did not want my family to split up. I did not want to join the statistics as a failed marriage. I knew that it would be devastating for my children, so I recommended we seek help, but he refused. So, I put on a brave front, hid and suppressed my emotions from my children, and accepted his decision to leave because my marriage was indeed miserable.

I decided that, if he did not want to be with me, I did not want to be with anyone who no longer wanted me. I had learned from my previous relationships that, if a man does not want to be with me, there is nothing I can do to change that, so it is better to work on getting over it and moving on. I guess I never understood why women try to force men to be with them when men have told them and made it crystal clear that they do not want to be with them. I do not want to be with anyone who does not want to be with me. Listen, women, if a man tells you he does not want to be with you, please accept it and move on. No, I did not say that it would be easy. It is not easy, but it is indeed necessary for you to move on because, if you can't let it go, if you can't let him go, then you cannot move forward. Don't be that woman who keeps holding on to a man who is not worth holding on to. If a man does not add value to your life, if you are not a priority in his life, if you are just a mere afterthought or booty call to him, please get over it and move on. The man you are with should add to your life and not stress you out. You are worth more. Do not devalue yourself.

It is much more difficult to let him go when he is your husband because there are usually children and property involved. But it is still necessary for you to let him go. Why would you even want to be with someone who has told you that he does not want to be with you? Oh, I can hear it now. Oh, girl, he didn't mean it. Um … girl, yes, he did. He said it, didn't he? I don't know why women think that they can change a man and mold him into what they want. Stop it! We can't! You deserve better than that. Everyone deserves to be loved, wanted, and needed.

I had to finally acknowledge that, during the last three years of my sexless marriage, we were no longer connecting on any level. I cried myself to sleep many nights (far too many to count) because my husband did not want me. How did I know that? Well, he told me he did not want me.

I questioned God and wanted to know what I had done so badly in my life that I deserved to be in a miserable marriage. Even though my husband did not love me anymore, I still loved him and refused to hate him. Why? I was taught as a child by my preacher parents not to hate. Because of that teaching and belief, I don't understand how people end up hating—I mean venomously hating—their spouses when they are the ones who chose the persons who became the mothers or fathers of their children.

I was deeply in love with my husband, so much so that, when he would go out of town on a business trip, I would pray that God would return him safely home to me. I couldn't bear the thought of living without him. When he took ill with complications from diabetes, I put him in the shower and washed him when he was unable to take care of himself. I slept on the sofa when his body ached all over and the slightest of movement in bed would cause him discomfort and pain. That is what a wife is supposed to do—in sickness and in health, right? In an effort to try to save our marriage, I tried to communicate with my husband to let him know the areas I felt we needed to work on. Yes, I said *we*. I will not put all of the blame on my husband. It takes two to tango. I am not perfect, and there were areas I needed to work on. However, he rejected the idea of getting counseling and told me that he would never touch me again and that he hated me. Although he may have said these awful things to me out of anger, I believed him. I believed him because I felt it every day. I was miserable. There was no affection in our relationship and very little communication. Communication only revolved around the girls and finances.

So, at the age of forty-four, I found myself starting all over again with two daughters. I felt abandoned because I had hoped that I would grow old with my husband, and we would be together until the end of times. How naïve was I? Filled with anger, my husband bitterly told me that no man was going to want me with two children. The impact of all of this on my daughters weighed very heavily on me, so I had to develop a plan.

Principle One
Let *IT* Go: Whatever *IT* Is
He who forgives ends the quarrel.
—African Proverb

You would think that, after being treated so badly and experiencing several bouts of domestic violence, I would be bitter and hateful. But I am not. I believe in letting go. I have learned from the scriptures "Dearly beloved, avenge not yourselves, but rather give place unto wrath: for it is written, Vengeance is mine; I will repay, saith the Lord" (Romans 12:19 King James Version). Some people call it karma. The Bible also states you reap what you sow. So, you have to be careful how you treat others.

You've heard the phrase, "what goes around comes around." It is just not worth it to seek revenge or to try to get someone back for doing something to you. Choose to direct that negative energy into something positive, and you will get a better outcome. When you hold on to negative things, they can control your life—take over your life. They can actually consume your life if you let them. The ability to let go is a powerful tool that you can use to accomplish your goals. Holding on to negativity impedes your chances of reaching your destiny. Letting it go means eliminating everything that blocks your path. It may be your wife, husband, daughter, son, mother, father, sister, brother, or any vice—such as alcohol, drugs, or sex.

It is so important to let it go, because if you don't, whatever is troubling you can have a negative impact on your life, your family, and your goals. I had to learn that letting go is easier said than done. I was tested when I was notified that my brother had unexpectedly died in his sleep. Over the years, he'd had bouts with drugs, and as a result, his brain was affected. He would have weird thoughts, see things that weren't there, and do things that were out of the norm. When he was ready for help, we aided him in getting the mental health assistance he needed to become somewhat normal again. He saw many medical and mental health professionals and was prescribed medications to keep him stable. He was progressing very well. In fact, he was in the best shape my family and I had seen in a long time. After his treatments and care at the group home, the next step was to get him an apartment so that he could live on his own again. Unfortunately, that did not come to fruition. Even though, to this day, I do not understand his death, I had to let it go. Sometimes we may lose a loved one (too soon) and not understand the loss. We may even question god. This can consume us, if we continue to hold on to it.

Some things are simply out of your control. Letting go of whatever it is gives you the power to release the negative and bad energy in your life that can prevent you from moving forward toward your destiny.

Many of you are probably holding on to things that someone said about you or to you or did to you decades ago, but yet you are still holding a grudge. If you have had a bad relationship with a family member, friend, or work associate that is preventing you from seeing beyond the issue and conflict, I urge you to find a way to let it go. Even if the person does not apologize for what he or she did to you, it is important that you forgive and free yourself from the negative energy the relationship creates. Let it go, whatever it is, so that you can reach your destiny.

Principle Two
Self-Assess: *WOMAN* in the Mirror

He who knows others is clever; he who
knows himself is enlightened.
—Lao-Tzu, Chinese philosopher

There are so many women who go through life and do not know
their worth. I thought I knew the value of my life, but during my
teenage years, as do many young ladies, I experienced a time of
confusion, depression, and awkwardness. I felt that no one would
miss me if I were not there.

There was a person, Roy Seavey Campbell—aka Soul Papa—a
local radio personality in DC who mentored me and two of my
siblings as singers. I developed a close friendship with Soul Papa,
and he would talk with me and provide me advice and guidance.
One day, I was feeling down because both of my sisters, who were
just one and two years older than I, decided to take a different
course in life. I figured that, if they could do that, so could I, but
Soul Papa reminded me of how smart I was and how I needed to
stay in school to prepare for my future. We did not have just one
conversation, but many conversations, accompanied on my part by
many tears and many doubts. He was easy to talk to and provided
the guidance I needed at that time. He was a great mentor and the
reason I pursued communication studies in college.

Written by Dr. Theresa Poussaint

Through this process of communicating with Soul Papa, I realized my worth as a person. In my senior year of high school, Soul Papa was murdered. It was big news in DC, and they never found his killers. The newspaper stated that it had something to do with payola—recording artists paying radio stations and radio personalities to play their music on the air. He was kidnapped at gunpoint and executed. It was so tragic, and I and thousands of others were devastated. He had positively impacted my life so much that I wrote a poem about him that was recited over the airwaves and printed in the newspaper. Soul Papa is gone but not forgotten.

It amazes me that so many people do not know who they are—they only think they do—and what their purpose in life really is. It was during my MBA studies that I learned the most about myself. The course was filled with self-assessments along the way. There were tests for basic personality, motivation insights, communications, leadership and teams, power and conflict, decision making, and listening skills. There were also assessments for ethics, trust, and how to handle change. Understanding yourself and truly knowing who you are can be eye-opening.

Understanding your personality, triggers, and pressure points will allow you to develop skills that can help manage behaviors that are not effective to resolving conflicts and issues in your life and relationships. Thinking that you have all the answers and you are not the problem is naïve. There is always room for improvement in our self-development. One thing I learned to manage was the stress in my life. I learned not to worry about or hold onto things that are not under my control.

Principle Three
Have a Plan: Know Where *YOU* Are Going

If you don't care where you are going,
any road will get you there.
—Anonymous

When my husband told me he was leaving me, I had to come up with a plan. I was nearing the completion of my undergraduate studies and was in the process of positioning myself to become head of household due to my husband's struggle with the effects of diabetes. Come to find out after the separation, he thought I was getting my degree and preparing to leave him. This proved to me that he did not know me as well as I thought he did. I had made a promise to God with my wedding vows, and I had no intention of divorcing. However, I believed that God would not want me to live overshadowed by physical and mental abuse.

Now that I was facing the reality of having to take care of my daughters with or without the support of their father, I knew that it was important to have a plan. I decided to finish up my degree and then pursue an advanced degree so that I could compete for better positions and more money in the job market. This was my choice. I could have chosen to go into a state of depression, have a pity party, and encourage everyone to feel sorry for me because my husband left me. But I decided that I would be strong and focus on my daughters and their well-being. I chose not to worry about myself and my wants. Instead, I chose to accept his leaving as an opportunity that was prepared for me to finally have some peace in my life. I did not harbor any negative feelings or anger. Instead, I chose to turn the negative thoughts into positive thoughts. Actually, I felt a sense of relief and freedom.

Don't sit back and wait for things to happen; be proactive and make things happen. Having short-term and long-term goals is critical for mapping out where you want to be in the future. I developed a personal mission statement and used it as a guide to accomplish the things I wanted to do. I still use it today. It allows me to stay focused on working on areas of my life that needed improvement.

Personal Mission Statement

I will do my best to balance career and family since both are important to me.

I will be a self-starting individual who exercises initiative in accomplishing my life's goals.

I will seek and merit divine help so I can maintain focus and succeed in every aspect of my life.

I will listen twice as much as I speak.

I will maintain a positive attitude and a sense of humor.

I will obtain the counsel of others.

I will never compromise with honesty.

I will make my home a place where my family, friends, and I find joy, comfort, and peace.

I will exercise wisdom in what to teach my children to eat, read, see, and do at home.

I will teach my children to love, learn, laugh, and develop their unique talents.

I will act on situations and opportunities, rather than to be acted upon.

I will keep myself free from addictive and destructive habits.

I will develop habits that free me from old labels and limits, and that will expand my capabilities and choices.

I will not fear making mistakes, but fear only the absence of creative, constructive, and corrective responses to those mistakes.

I will seek financial independence over time.

I will make my wants subject to my needs and my means.

I will keep myself free from consumer debt except for long-term home loans.

I will spend less than I earn and regularly save or invest part of my income.

Written by Dr. Theresa Poussaint

I will use what money and talents I have to make life more enjoyable for others through volunteering services and charitable giving.

I will be sincere yet decisive.

I will value the rights, freedoms, and responsibilities of our democratic society and be a concerned and informed citizen, involved in the political process to ensure my voice is heard and my vote is counted.

I will plan tomorrow's work today and develop one new proficiency a year.

Principle Four
Lead by Example: *THEY* Are Watching You
Live as you wish your kids would.
—Anonymous

When you decide to have a child, you are responsible for raising that child to be a productive member of society. What we do as parents influences those we raise. Leading by example is one of the most profound ways you can teach your children. Many parents operate in the realm of "do as I say and not as I do." That is a hypocritical way of parenting. It was very important for me to teach my daughters how to become independent-thinking, self-reliant, confident, moral, and self-motivating women. Hopefully my teachings were able to minimize or entirely eliminate the possibility of my daughters being objectified by men—being used for sex and devalued.

I want to make sure that, when they choose to be with a man, they will ensure that he—"the man"—is, in fact, worthy of them. My daughters needed to know their self-worth and value. I know that it is a double-edged sword because I am probably making it difficult for them to "find" the right man because their standards will be very high and they will choose a mate wisely, but I am also preventing them from being "used" by men. Men have a greater tendency to think with their heads; that is, not the ones attached to their necks. I would rather err on the side of caution even though it might make it more difficult for them to find a mate.

These are lessons I learned throughout my life. It is not until you have actually experienced life that you can reflect and understand the causes and ramifications of your actions. What causes you to give yourself to so many men? Loneliness? Emptiness? Low self-esteem? Many do it because they did not grow up with a father or father figure. Many do it because women are emotional creatures and just want to be loved. Almost for the same reason, some women choose to intentionally get pregnant and have a child. They believe that they can get and keep a man that way. Wrong. They just want something (the baby) to love and to love them back. Wrong again. That is not a sensible and wise reason to get pregnant and have a baby.

I chose not to bring various men into my life and my home while I had two impressionable daughters at home. You know—the men who end up being referred to as Uncle So and So.

In her book, *On My Mother's Prayers: Save the Children*, Myrtice Walters Stephens wrote, "Our background and circumstances may have influenced who we are, but we are responsible for who we become." So, even if you come from a dysfunctional upbringing— the majority of us do—we do not have to be dysfunctional ourselves. For example, as the youngest of nine children, I looked to my siblings as role models. Unfortunately, some of my siblings did not always make wise choices that were worthy of following. However, I learned from their behavior and chose not to do some of things I saw them do. Two of my brothers and two of my sisters have passed away, I believe way too soon. And in my view, their early and untimely deaths were preventable.

My eldest brother was only forty-six years old when he went into a diabetic coma and died. He abused his body with drugs and alcohol, and he failed to monitor his sugar levels and take his medication in a timely fashion. One day he passed out, and his brain was deprived of oxygen for too long before he was found. He was in a coma for months before he succumbed.

My other brother died at the age of fifty-eight mysteriously in his sleep. Unfortunately, he abused drugs and, as a result, suffered from mental health issues. He did not take care of himself either, the way he should have.

One of my sisters was only fifty years old when she passed away from lung cancer. She was a smoker and actually knew that she was terminal but decided that she did not want anyone to know about her fatal prognosis. One day I received the call that she was taken to the hospital where she died shortly thereafter.

My other sister was sixty-one years old when she passed away from sclerosis of the liver. She was an alcoholic and always said and believed you have to die from something, so why not alcohol, which she enjoyed very much.

Remember, your children are watching you! It is important that you *show* them—not just *tell* them—how to take care of themselves and how to choose to do the right things. Teach them to be moral citizens of good character. I learned from my parents and my siblings. I learned that life is full of choices. What we choose to do and say and how we choose to live will determine our destiny.

After the divorce, Max became too ill to live alone, and he had to move into a nursing home where he was the youngest resident at only fifty-two years old. I visited him often, sometimes multiple times a week. I took him food on my lunch break and took the girls on the weekends to visit him. I bought and washed his clothes and was there when one of his legs was amputated. He was the father of my daughters, and it was important for me not to abandon him even though I felt he had abandoned me. I chose to do the opposite of what was expected.

Max suffered greatly during his illness and came close to death several times. He was able to reflect on his life with me. Before he died, he said, "You are a good person and a great mother. Please forgive me for all of the things I did to you". And, I told him, I already did. After his death, as a co-signer on his apartment, I was responsible for all of his worldly possessions. So, it all came back to me and I gifted everything to our daughters.

Principle Five
Persevere: *DON'T* Give Up

The race is not given to the swift nor the
strong, but to he who endures until the end.
—Ecclesiastes 9:11

I completed three degrees after my divorce. It has not been easy, but I accepted the challenge and persevered. I know that, if I can do it, anyone can do it. Shortly after my husband left, I graduated and received my bachelor's degree in communication studies. I thought that was a major milestone, and I didn't really think about going any further than that at that time. However, when I attended commencement, I noticed something. First, I noticed there was another group of graduates, and their regalia looked much better than mine. They had different colors around their hoods, and their caps were velvet. They indeed looked more scholarly. They were the master's degree candidates. The second thing I noticed was that the majority of the people who walked across the stage to receive that degree looked like me. They were African American women. I told myself at that moment, *Well, if they can earn a master's degree, certainly I can to.* They did not look as if they had any special quality that was different than mine. So, the next semester I enrolled in the MBA two-and-one-half-year program.

I knew that obtaining an MBA would put me in a better position to compete in the job market, and it would assist me in advancing my career. So, I sat down and talked with my daughters to let them know that I would be making some sacrifices as I pursued my degree. I told them that, after I graduated, I would make up for not spending a lot of time with them doing things such as taking them to the movies and the mall. I knew I would have to sacrifice all of that and focus on my coursework. They understood my desire and my quest and did not complain too much.

While I went through the process of earning my MBA, life went on, which also meant life events -still occurred. Another of my siblings passed away. Something was wrong with my sister. She wouldn't eat and she didn't want to see anyone. She was rushed to the hospital on a Wednesday and she died two days later. The doctors showed us the MRI of her brain and lungs and said that she had been sick for a long time. They were shocked when we told them that we had no idea. When she died, I was so upset with her because she had not told us she was ill. If she had told us, we would have done anything and everything to save her life, but I guess her lung cancer was in an advanced stage, and she knew that there was nothing we could do. That was so brave of her, and I miss her dearly. It appears that many years of smoking cigarettes took a toll on her lungs. I don't know if I could have faced the certainty of death as calmly or as logically as she did. Perhaps she had accepted her fate and positioned her mind to not fight the inevitable. She was only fifty years old. But the kicker is that she knew she was dying but decided not to tell anyone. I suppose this was actually a smart thing to do because it saved my parents the heartache of dealing with her illness for longer than they needed to do. She was so smart. My feelings about her not telling us changed over time. Time does heal all wounds.

However, there is one thing I wish I had paid more attention to. I remember visiting her a few months prior to her fiftieth birthday. We just talked in general, and when I was getting ready to leave, she said, "What are you all going to do for my fiftieth birthday?" I said, "I don't know." She said, "I'm just kidding." I asked, "Are you going to have a pool party here?" She said, "Oh, I don't know." In hindsight, I wish I had done more to celebrate her milestone birthday. She was born on the fourth of July. I think she was trying to tell me that she wanted that celebration to be her last family event. She died two months before her fifty-first birthday.

Even though my sister's death was a devastating point in my life, I did not give up on my studies and did not use her death as an excuse to give up on my MBA. I persevered. In fact, one evening when a conference call was scheduled for the class, I contacted my professor and informed him that my sister had died. Even though the family was at my sister's home mourning and making arrangements for the funeral, I thought of my class. I went to my car and dialed in. When my professor heard my voice on the call, he was shocked that I was participating. The one thing I understand about death is that life goes on. The loved one may have passed on, but those left behind must continue on their paths. So, even though I had lost my sister, I knew that I had to continue my studies.

Another event occurred that could have prevented me from completing my MBA. During the final course of the program, I got really sick. I had a cold, the cold turned into the flu, the flu turned into bronchitis, and the bronchitis turned into pneumonia. That was the worst I had ever felt. I felt as if I was dying. I called my doctor to make an appointment. After the doctor examined me, she told me that I needed to go to the emergency room right away because my blood pressure, temperature, pulse rate, and respiration rate were all irregular. I told her that I had driven myself to the appointment, but she told me that I could not drive. I called my sister, who worked just across the street from the doctor's office, and she took me to the emergency room. The emergency room doctor examined me and told me that I had pneumonia. In fact, he told me that my lungs were so congested that, if it were not for my young age of forty-five, I would have died. In other words, if someone older were in my condition, the condition would have been terminal. I was admitted to the hospital and put on a series of antibiotics and fluids. I was out of commission for about ten days and fell behind in my studies. As I got better, I continued with my coursework. It took me a while to get back into the swing of things. In fact, the first paper I submitted to my professor after my bout with pneumonia was not up to par. My professor allowed me to improve it, and I received a passing grade. He noted on the paper "Welcome back!" I worked diligently to catch up and stay with my fellow students. We had started together, and I worked hard and did not give up so I could finish and graduate on schedule with them.

Also, during this time, my ex-husband was a resident in a nursing home. I decided I would be the better person and show my daughters that I would still do what I could do for their dad. I often heard from family members and friends' comments like "Why are you taking care of him?" and "You are better than me, girl. After what he did to you, I don't know why you still care." When my husband left me, although I tried to remain strong and be strong for my daughters, I was devastated. I felt rejected and felt like a failure because my marriage had failed. But I was also relieved because I no longer had to live with someone who hated me, who did not want to touch me. That is what he told me, and that is what he displayed over the last three years of our marriage. So, yes, there was a sense of relief. We split the assets and put the house on the market. Before he moved out, he had been ill and was weak. After this brief period of illness, he got better and made his move. He had planned it and had everything lined up.

Shortly after he moved into his new apartment, he began living the lifestyle of a bachelor; at least, that is what it looked like from the outside. He agreed to voluntarily give me support money for the girls. As his newfound bachelorhood days kicked in, his funds for child support became scarce. It appeared as though everything else was a priority, and the girls were not. I guess it was a case of out of sight out of mind. It got to the point that he stopped contributing altogether. He thought that, just because he took care of the girls when they went to visit him once or twice a month, he was doing his part. We made the arrangement that he would get the girls every other weekend, but unfortunately, he did not live up to that either. So, I chose to file the papers for child support. This was not an easy decision. I actually struggled with it because I did not want to anger him or make him hate me even more. As I sat there at the courthouse with other women, I listened to their stories. One after the other, they talked about how the fathers of their children were no good, dodging addresses, and working under the table so they could hide their income. It made me feel a little better because it made me realize that my husband was not like theirs. I did feel that I was doing a disservice to my girls by not getting their father to contribute to their well-being. I did not make them by myself, so I should not have to be responsible for taking care of them by myself.

Written by Dr. Theresa Poussaint

When I returned to the court for our hearing, Max showed up while I was sitting in the waiting area. He was not happy to see me. We had independently met with a mediator to see how much he would be able to contribute. I had all of my employment information and so did he. However, I was informed that they could not hold him to anything because he had also brought a notice from his attorney indicating that he had filed for bankruptcy. What the what? There was nothing they could do. So, the mediator encouraged me to ask Max to agree to $100 a month for each child. At least it was something. He paid for a while but then fell behind. The state notified me that he was in arrears for about $13,000. He had fallen behind due to his deteriorating health, which caused him to miss work.

His driver's license was even suspended due to nonpayment of child support. At this time, although he did not want me, he needed me again. He asked me to release him from having to pay the child support that was in arrears so that he could get his driver's license back because he needed to get back and forth to his doctor appointments. So, I went to court and had the debt dissolved. He was so grateful that I had done this for him. The judge asked me if I understood that, if I dissolved this debt, I would not be able to go after him again for it. I told her that I indeed understood. I felt that, because his health was deteriorating and he was unable to work, it would be futile to try to get any financial support from him. In the meantime, I was pursuing my master's degree to better position myself to be able to take care of my girls and myself without any financial support from their father.

I was offered and accepted a position that gave me an opportunity to complete a doctorate degree. I took advantage of this opportunity so that I could position myself to be able to teach at any university. Most universities require a terminal degree, so when I earned my doctorate, I would be able to compete with other applicants. I was also thinking about what I could do after I retired from working—teach. Teaching is my passion, and I have no intentions of retiring. My goal is to be active in my retirement years, exercising my brain in academia. Again, I had to sit down with my daughters to inform them that I was pursuing another degree and that I would have to make more sacrifices. This time I would be graduating with my doctorate the same year my youngest daughter would be graduating from high school.

The doctoral degree program was much different than the master's program, and it required a three-year commitment. One of my mentors, Dr. Frank, gave me great advice and told me to take it one course at a time, one assignment at a time. He advised me not to look too far ahead because it would become too overwhelming. So, I took his advice to heart, and it worked. However, in the final course of the program, I experienced déjà vu. I was not ready to present my dissertation. I had not dedicated enough time to my dissertation due to personnel changes in my department at work. My staff had been reduced, but the workload had remained the same, so the job became overwhelming.

I knew that I had a cushion of one semester that would enable me to graduate with my fellow students. So, when I started that last course in the spring, I was more than ready. I did not slow down. I dedicated my weekends to my dissertation. I went to my office and worked for eight to ten hours on Saturdays and Sundays until I was satisfied that I had a strong dissertation and I had developed my thesis and argument and was able to support that argument with my findings. It paid off, because when I defended and presented my dissertation, I received great feedback from the doctoral faculty and rave reviews from doctoral students. Earning my doctorate degree was one of the most challenging aspects of my life. But I persevered and did it. I finished and graduated with my fellow students.

On the way to commencement, my daughter Felicity looked at me and said, "Mom, I am so proud of you. There is one thing I know about you for sure and that is, when you say you are going to do something, you do it." I told her, "You know why? One of the reasons is that I know that you are watching me."

It is important to lead by example and show your children what is possible. I know that, when Felicity goes to college or decides to pursue anything, she will go all the way. She will press through the tough times and won't give up.

I did it time and time again. Even though it took me many years just to get my bachelor's degree, I loved academia. I was put on this earth to teach. That is my true calling. I did not give up. Age is just a number. While many may earn their doctorate degrees when they are in their twenties, I earned mine when I was in my fifties. I am still Dr. Poussaint.

It seems that I was challenged the most, when I was at the cusp of accomplishing a goal. Just before I earned my bachelor's degree, my husband left me and asked for a divorce. Just before I earned my MBA, I got deathly sick and my sister died. Just before I earned my doctorate, I was overwhelmed on my job and had to become laser focused to finish. And, just before I finished writing this book, my 32-year-old daughter Cordelia unexpectedly died.

To My Loving Daughter:

Cordelia my heart is hurting because I miss you so much. I told you I wanted you to play your violin at my funeral which means you were supposed to bury me. To me, this is the wrong order, but my faith is not shaken and I know that God knows what is best. For the first eight years of your life, your dad and I had you all to ourselves and we poured so much love into you. I know you had a difficult time living without your dad, but I also know that you are now at peace with him. You are so much like your father; your height; your taste of art and culture; your love of music, specifically Johann Sebastian Bach and Classical Baroque Music, and your love of your sister Felicity. I am going to miss your beautiful face, your quick wit, your bombastic presence, your laughter, our intellectual and thought-provoking conversations, our discussions on literature, astronomy, religion and politics, and our Jeopardy and Wheel of Fortune competitions. Until we meet again my beautiful daughter, rest in eternal peace. Mom

Life goes on even after traumatic or challenging experiences. It is up to you to decide how you will deal with life. You can either allow yourself to be held back from reaching your destiny, or you can defy the odds and persevere.

That is my message to you who are reading my book: You don't have to be filled with anger, hate, and negativity. You can choose to be different and show your children that they can choose to be better persons.

Make a concerted effort to choose to:

Let *IT* Go: Whatever *IT* Is

Self-Assess: *WOMAN* in the Mirror

Have a Plan: Know Where *YOU* Are Going

Lead by Example: *THEY* Are Watching You

Persevere: *DON'T* Give Up

Following these principles will lead you into a calm, fulfilling, and stress-free life. Remember, you have *The Power to Navigate Your Destiny.*

CPSIA information can be obtained
at www.ICGtesting.com
Printed in the USA
BVHW030214200121
598211BV00010B/162

9 781480 897939